A World War II Holiday Scrapbook

Also by Gail Kittleson

In Times Like These
With Each New Dawn
A Purpose True
All for the Cause
Until Then
Kiss Me Once Again
In This Together
Catching Up With Daylight

Also by Cleo Lampos

A Mother's Song
Dust Between the Stitches
Riding the Rails to Home
Piecing Fabrics~Mending Lives

Also by Kittleson & Lampos

The Food that held the World Together

A World War II Holiday Scrapbook
Copyright © 2020
Gail Kittleson & Cleo Lampos

ISBN: 978-1-952474-23-1

Cover concept and design by David Warren.

All rights reserved. No part of this book may be reproduced, stored in a retrieval system, or transmitted in any form or by any means—electronic, mechanical, photocopy, recording or otherwise—without the prior written permission of the publisher. The only exception is brief quotations for review purposes.

Published by WordCrafts Press
Cody, Wyoming 82414
www.wordcrafts.net

A World War II Holiday Scrapbook

Gail Kittleson & Cleo Lampos

WordCrafts

Contents

Dedication 1
Introduction 2
Christmas in North Platte 4
Mail Call at Christmas 7
Wartime Christmas on the Farm 10
The Yule Tide Tree 12
Salute to Imagination 17
Baseball and World War II 22
Shared Joys 24
Celebrating with the Roosevelts 27
Popping Up Some Comfort 32
Deploying Santa and the Reindeer 35
Giving from the Heart 39
Innovative Christmas Gifts 42
The Fragrance of Yule Tide 46
The Red Cross Christmas Parcels 52
When War Changes the Pulpit 58
That Homesick Feeling 63

Dedication

To those who seek to learn from the lessons history provides. May these insights deepen our appreciation for those who have gone before us through difficult times and bring us closer to our roots.

Introduction

By definition the word *nostalgic*, with so many good-byes involved, goes hand-in-hand with the World War II era.

From the moment President Roosevelt announced the Pearl Harbor attack, even isolated corners of the nation experienced change. In little towns all across this great land, families said good-bye to sons as they went off to a brutal war.

Many believed that, with Americans now involved, the war would be over by the next Christmas. But this was not to be. In fact, many families would not spend the holidays with their deployed loved ones until 1946 or '47.

As the months passed, constant new product rationing made typical gift giving difficult or impossible. As more companies transformed their factories for the war effort, holiday gifts reverted to the "homemade" sort.

Before December 7, 1941, one woman recalls receiving packages from her older British cousin, whose country was already in duress. This lady unraveled old sweaters to create tiny doll sweaters and dresses and mailed them to relatives in the United States. She said she did this to "pass the time," and we can well imagine the children's delight when the mailman brought this gift.

As the war droned on, packages were more likely sent from

Introduction

the U.S. to England. Brown paper-wrapped boxes containing food items made their way to hungry families.

In the States, industrious folks turned to lessons learned during Depression times. Do your best with what you have. Make do. Innovate. Such a unique time in our nation's history, with untold stories still surfacing seventy-five years later.

We share some of these here. It's healthy to embrace this era's spirit. During this past year, the United States has engaged in another war—a battle with disease. May the actions and ingenuity of the Greatest Generation emanate hope for our own trying times.

Chapter 1

Christmas in North Platte

The U.S. Army soldiers riding the Union Pacific train on Christmas Day, 1941, predictably felt homesick. For many, this holiday centered about traditions and family. Back at home. The coldness of the snowy Nebraska landscape brought melancholy to even the stiffest upper lip of recruits plucked recently from high school.

Then the troop train stopped for fifteen minutes in North Platte. The uniformed lads disembarked into the hospitality of a community of people. Their goal? Launching a canteen to greet the troop trains. Rae Wilson, the organizer, and a small group of volunteers distributed holiday treats and gifts in their first contribution to building morale during war.

From 1941 through 1945, the 1918 Union Pacific Depot sparkled with donated decorations that put Christmas spirit into the hearts of the enlisted men. Small gifts of handkerchiefs, combs, socks, playing cards, and "just the thing you would send your boy; that is the thing that would please some other mother's son."[1]

The wrapped bundles fascinated the men. "They picked up presents in both hands and, laughing and surprised, shook them, smelled them and felt of them until they were able to decide which present they wanted to keep."[2] These 25 to 50 cent items appeared to be priceless to men too old for Santa.

But the homemade food filling the tables took the troops' breath away. Having survived for weeks on C-Rations or mess hall hash, the piles of roast beef sandwiches, trays of hard-boiled eggs, cookies, cake, and coffee overwhelmed their senses. And hand-sized popcorn balls made with molasses. The food smelled delectable and tasted delicious. Almost as good as Mom's home-cooking. Girls with baskets of fruit circulated among the soldiers. Cigarettes, nuts, and candy tempted them to load their pockets with goodies.

Music filled the air with a mixture of the popular tunes of the day, Christmas carols, and, especially, "Happy Holidays." The men sang and ate at the same time, swaying to the beat of "Tuxedo Junction" or "In the Mood." Some danced with the teenagers who enjoyed a lively workout. It always amazed the volunteers how fifteen minutes lifted the morale of the military.

The older women boarded the hospital cars that held wounded and recuperating GIs. As the war progressed, the

pain that these mothers bore when they handed magazines, playing cards and food to the bandaged soldiers hid behind their smiles. Each GI looked to them like a brother, son, or neighbor. They treated these men with particular kindness, and silently prayed for their recovery.

The North Platte Canteen served some six million GIs over the next 51 months and one week. The existence of the canteen was actually due to a mistake. Shortly after Pearl Harbor, on December 17, the town gathered to greet the train carrying Company D of the North Platte-based Nebraska National Guard to deployment out East. They had assembled food and gifts for "their boys."

Instead, Company D of the Kansas National Guard disembarked onto the depot platform. After a few awkward moments, the folks of North Platte showered the Kansas Guardsmen with presents and treats because they realized that America's boys were "their boys." The dream greeting every troop train in North Platte was born.

On Christmas Day, 1941, volunteers answered the encrypted message on the party line: "The coffee pot is on." They served about 300 men on five troop trains carrying vets back home—a legacy of giving moral support to the troops began on Christmas Day and ended when the war finished. The folks of North Platte embodied the Christmas message as they sent the troops into a world of darkness with the warmth of their blessings.

"Celebrating Christmas at the Canteen." by Todd Von Kampen, December 22, 2019, todd.vonkampen@nptelegraph.com

1. page 7

2. page 10

Chapter 2

Mail Call at Christmas

"Christmas Greetings! May the New Year hold for you the best of everything that peace and freedom bring."
~Message on WWII Navy Christmas card

The troops of WWII relied on hand-written letters to communicate to loved ones back on the Home Front. Mail call was an important part of a military person's existence, and a reason for higher morale. Letters bearing the penmanship

of a loved one, packages and recordings were the most popular items received.

During the war, specific Christmas cards were created to send to those stationed across the oceans on foreign  land. These cards became the gift that kept on giving hope and served as lights at the end of a long, dark tunnel. Some carried these cards throughout their time overseas as a source of encouragement.

Hallmark Cards used the slogan, "keep 'em happy with mail." Their cards needed to be sent by October 15th to ensure delivery near Christmas, and the same was true for packages. These mailed items were portable pieces of home that cheered a fatigued GI after a day of fighting or arriving at a new destination. The cards and boxes took the men from their stressful situation to a thousand miles away where they envisioned their families enjoying a sense of calm.

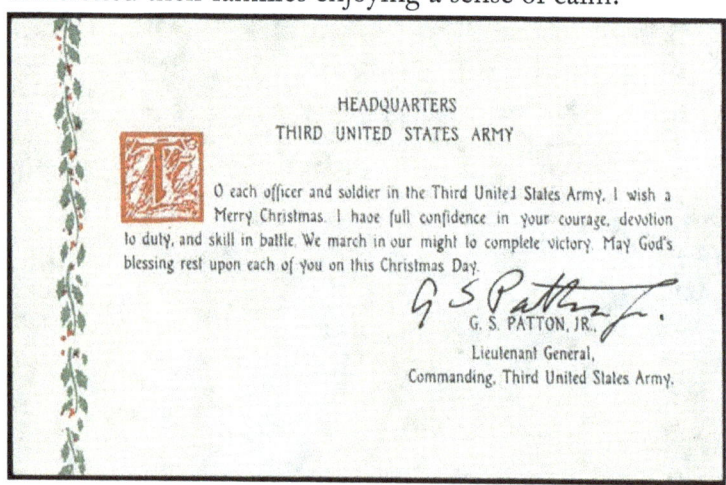

The typical cards carried the red, white, and blue color combo which reinforced the patriotic spirit of the sender. An Uncle Sam or Santa Claus dressed as a soldier amused the receiving GI. Other cards featured a wreath and a "Merry Christmas" with space for a personal message.

In 1944, General George Patton sent cards out to his troops reminding each of them of the full confidence he had in their strength and dedication to victory.

Christmas cards. They remind us that at Yule Tide, all roads lead home.

Chapter 3

Wartime Christmas on the Farm

It wasn't much, maybe, but this tree sufficed to bring smiles to this little eighteen-month old toddler and her brother. They had a mother who cared enough to produce a Christmas tree for them for the holidays.

That year, she may have had to scrounge the ditches around their farm place to find it, but what mattered was that she made the effort. And in the process, she introduced them to the spirit of Christmas.

From her meager supply, she produced some cheap tinsel and a few colored baubles to decorate this simple tree. She

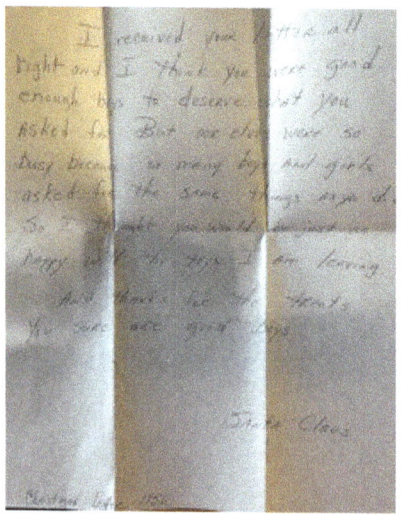

baked some cinnamon bread and slipped a few presents under the boughs to "make" Christmas for her brood.

The going might have been tough, but they had a roof over their heads, chickens, cows, and pigs for food, and garden produce preserved on the basement shelves. Down the road lived Grandma

Wartime Christmas on the Farm

and Grandpa, if worse came to worse. Let winter blow in with its fierce storms! Let the winds howl! This mother would keep her family warm with stories and songs. "I'll be home for Christmas," she'd sing. "I'm dreaming of a white Christmas," she'd hum.

And the colored lights on that straggly little specimen sparkled as brightly as any in a wealthy family's home. "We enjoyed a *Charlie Brown* tree before they were invented," says the grown-up little girl in the photograph.

Chapter 4

The Yule Tide Tree

"Nothing ever seems too bad, too hard, or too sad when you've got a Christmas tree in the living room."
~Nora Roberts

After the deprivation of the Great Depression, the availability to decorate a Christmas tree in every home took over just before the war put a kibosh on this one tradition. The festiveness of decorating the branches of a freshly cut pine tree, still shining from stars and snow, smelling of resin—who wouldn't be taken in?

By inhaling a lungful of the air around such a tree, the soul filled with wintery night goodness. But as the war dragged on, such extravagances lessened for urban dwellers.

Real trees were in short supply. A lack of manpower to cut trees down, and then the shortage of railroad space to ship them when a country needed to move military materials by road and rail made pine trees out of the reach of many city folks. But parents determined to give their children some joy in the midst of rationing displayed creativity and determination.

The three Palombo sisters grew up in an Italian home on the south side of Chicago. In their family of six children, their hard-working father went to the tree lots scattered in the neighborhood to buy a tree. With the heirloom angel

The Yule Tide Tree

from Italy and decorations handed down through the decades, this family added bubble lights. The sisters recall Christmas as a magical time.

Helen Taylor lived in the Swedish section of Chicago's segregated neighborhoods. Her father waited until Christmas Day when the tree lots lowered the prices on the left-over pines.

"I'll give you so much for that stick over there."

Helen recalls the bargaining of her father as he pointed to a tree that was full on one side, flat on the other. In the end, he negotiated for two "half-trees." Then he pushed the pines onto the streetcar and headed home. A rope tied the trunks

together, forming a round, full decorative treasure. Popcorn chains and colorful paper glued to toilet rolls brought cheer to this family living in a storefront apartment.

For many, the new artificial and inexpensive trees solved the problem. Addis Brush Company produced brushes for cleaning toilets. When the WWII tree shortage hit, they geared up their brush-making machinery. Using a bottle brush, they created a small tree that mimicked the pine very well.

Cleo Lampos' family used their three-foot brush Christmas tree for decades as the main decoration in their home. In 1941, a five-foot American-made Visca artificial tree could be purchased for seventy-five cents—a real bargain!

During the war, the German and Japanese ornaments that had been purchased in a friendlier decade were disposed of or put away in an attic. The Corning Glass Company of New York began making glass ornament products. Ribbons and bow material were very scarce, so frugal use of these colorful fabrics was needed.

Families painted, glittered, and hung pine cones and nuts. To create a snow effect on the tree, a box of Lux soap powder and two cups of water mixed and brushed onto branches provided a natural look.

Virginia Pulver of LeMars, Iowa, still remembers the decorations on her family Christmas tree during the war. Her parents sentimentally resurrected the old icicles they had made from the keyed coffee can lids. Paper chains linked from magazine images garlanded their tree. Year after year, Virginia's Great Depression parents carefully handled the annual decorations. "After all, this was the People's War, and we had to do all we could to survive."

Even the hospital wards in the field reflected the Christmas spirit with artificial or real trees. Nurses snipped tin from plasma cans to make stars to string from tent ceilings. Ration tins and foil wrapping ingeniously folded brought the glitter.

It was not uncommon for soldiers on the front lines to decorate random trees around them. They chopped them down to bring to their tents, or to the makeshift headquarters. Those in the Pacific theatre used palm trees to hang their shiny "found" items for ornaments.

Even a few branches draped with paper brought the melancholy for home and wistfulness for tradition to the hearts of GIs on active duty. Those GIs who ate in mess halls, canteens, or back in the States enjoyed a tree with as many trimmings as the situation allowed.

Blackout regulations were imposed on September 1, 1939, even before America declared war. All windows and doors were covered at night with curtains, cardboard, or paint to prevent the escape of even a glimmer of light to aid enemy aircraft. Strict compliance was observed. The moon glow that comforted so many into sleep lay on the other side of the bedroom wall as darkness descended on America.

Outdoor Christmas lights were banned on December 11, 1941. Community Christmas tree lighting ceremonies were postponed until after the war. The black-out on the West Coast, a dim-out in the East, and the rest of the nation under black out curtains left the stars as the only sparkle on Christmas Eve outside of the home.

But within the shelter of the walls of individual apartments, cabins, or houses, candles and lights glowed with an optimistic hope for the future. Christmas trees lights flickered sparkling patterns onto walls, ceilings, and floor with gleaming promise.

Taylor Caldwell summarizes: "And that, of course, is the message of Christmas. We are never alone. Not when the night is darkest, the wind coldest, the world seemingly most indifferent."

Chapter 5

Salute to Imagination

"Creativity is intelligence having fun.
~Albert Einstein

War affects everyone, even the children. The rationing of metal and rubber during World War II meant that toys using those materials became prohibited—except for the kids of wealthy parents.

The rest of the nation's kids needed toys that sparked their imagination and gave them hope. Thus, girls found presents under the tree that utilized their verbal and social skills.

Paper dolls made of an unrationed material provided nurses, soldiers in various uniforms, career women and mothers. The object was to clothe these figures with the numerous outfits cut from paper. Several young ladies gathered together could develop dialogue and drama with these stand-up cardboard people. All it took was a little ingenuity.

Cloth dolls and teddy bears created from socks elicited the nurturing spirits of youngsters. Imitating the voices of adults, children sang lullabies to these comforting, squishable friends.

In many cases, Grandpas took up the slack by going to their workshops. There, the master craftsmen built cradles and tables with chairs for their granddaughters and their dolls. A little paint combined with grandma's quilting touch and the presents drew gasps of approval from the little girls.

In that same workshop, fathers who were not deployed whittled toys for their boys from chunks of wood.

For preschoolers, wooden trucks with wheels and moveable parts proved to be successful toys pushing dirt in summer sand boxes. In the skilled hands of a woodcrafter, boats, arks, airplanes and wagons emerged from blocks of lumber. Even sleds for wintery slopes found their way from Grandpa's memory to his carving knife.

Eric Caddy recalls: "The best Christmas ever was when I

got the Tommy Gun that my father carved from firewood. It is still my best present ever."

Boys enjoyed lead soldiers, tin vehicles, and cap guns as Christmas presents. Their creativity led them to hours of play time with these small pieces on the kitchen table, living room rug, or the dirt out back.

Lionel Company sold the *Wartime Freight Train*, which was made of heavy-duty paper stock and needed assembly. Many toy manufacturers like Lionel converted their factories into facilities that produced wartime equipment. Even with the restrictions, Lionel engineered impressive moving train sets out of strong cardboard.

As a wartime child, Betty Zier lived in Chicago's south side. Like so many other children, she felt gratitude for the stocking filled with oranges, a banana, nuts, and hard candy. Anything else seemed to be extra. Her practical grandmother knitted sweaters for gifts for her and her siblings.

Frugal grandparents brought toys back to life. Kathy Vigus-Kolstad from Posen, Illinois, remembers that her grandmother would take a favorite stuffed toy and rehab it. She took it apart, washed the fabric, and re-stuffed the body. "Nice and clean, she checked the eyes and if one or both were missing, she replaced them with fancy buttons from her sewing box. Under the tree, it became sort of a new toy. We were happy."

Books have long liberated the imagination of children. During the war, favorites included: *Call it Courage, Rabbit Hill, Homer Price, Pippi in the South Seas, Misty of Chincoteague,* and *the Boxcar Children*. Literature taught the reader the message from *Les Misérables*, published during tumultuous Civil War times: "Even the darkest night will end, and the sun will rise."

Puzzles, playing cards, and board games met with wartime requirements. Chalkboards with colored chalk molded youngsters to take up the teaching profession years later. Wood-burning kits, crayons, and paint sets sold rapidly. Lincoln Logs, and tinker toys taught building skills. Creativity and imagination spiked during the war years because the toys needed grey matter charged with out-of-the-box thinking.

In a dark time, Christmas presents brought joy to children on the home front. Especially the delight of playing with the boxes.

"Laughter is timeless, imagination has no age, and dreams are forever," said Walt Disney.

Here, some parents have rigged up a fun ride for their sons. It took ingenuity to attach their sleds to the runners of an antique sleigh, but hours of winter fun resulted from their efforts. Imagine how the snow sprayed these delighted boys as they hung on for dear life!

This photograph may have been shot during the Christmas holidays—the sleds probably were used specimens, but who cared?

A New Building Mode

In the late 1930's, Halsam Products Company of Chicago introduced inter-locking toy bricks for children. Pressed from hardwood much like dominoes and equipped with a peg, socket and slot

Salute to Imagination

construction, these identical blocks replicated the brick layer's process in constructing a building.

In 1941, a new division of this company was called ELGO, after Hal Elliott and Samuel Goss, Jr. took the *El* from Elliott and the *Go* from Goss to form the name. Originally, they did the same thing with their first names to form *Halsam*.

To be precise, these injected mold plastics weren't available to the general public during the war because the company was too busy performing government contract work. But it wasn't long afterward that Greatest Generation children were delighting in a set for a birthday or Christmas.

It's important to note the unisex marketing employed by ELGO at this early date. Girls might be as likely to receive a set of these bricks as their male friends.

A little boy who played with ELGO sets grew to be a successful farmer, and his sister, who now stores them in her basement, adds a comment. "Elmo was always really careful with his things—we all were back then."

Note: if you're thinking there's too great a similarity between ELGO and LEGO, the ELGO blocks were created about ten years before the LEGO brand.

Chapter 6

Baseball and World War II

P lenty of American youths would have been happy to find a new baseball glove under the Christmas tree. Scooted up to the radio, they followed the major league games throughout the season, and rooted for their favorite teams.

And they knew about sacrifice from the players who ended up on ships or with the infantry overseas. One young player debuted in the minor leagues in 1943, hitting .396 his first season.

He'd have been drafted into the majors in '44, had it not been for his draft status.

During the next season, he served as a gunner's mate on the USS Bayfield during the Allied landings at Normandy. On this Navy rocket boat, he fired machine guns and launched rockets on the enemy dug in at Omaha Beach. A Purple Heart winner, he became a hero in every sense of the word.

Another successful player, Bob Feller, had amassed seventy-six wins in the three

Baseball and World War II

seasons leading up to the Pearl Harbor attack, but entered the Navy instead of accepting a $100,000 contract. Not satisfied to be used by the military to entertain troops, he enrolled in gunnery school and served during the Battle of the Philippine Sea aboard the USS Alabama.

Then there was the Boston Braves pitcher headed for his 400th win when he joined the army. In the Battle of the Bulge, Warren Spahn fought at the Ludendorff Bridge and earned a Purple Heart.

Another Detroit Tiger great, Hank Greenberg, eventually became a five-time All Star player, four-time American League home run leader, and two-time World Series Champion. But on the way to this career, this Hall-of-Famer was the first major league player to enlist, and lost four seasons to the war.

Due to a bomb blast as gas tanks blew up on a downed burning B-29, he lost his hearing and speaking ability for a time, but was able to return to his career after the war. So was another service member named Joe DiMaggio.

And because of these players' courage in serving their country, the All American Girls Professional League was born. No doubt, some girls were glad to find a baseball glove under the tree during the war years, as well.

Chapter 7

Shared Joys

Growing up during the war years, Eileen Jahr was blessed with a happy Scandinavian-American home. Her mother, a perfectionist, allowed no running inside the house, but her father got down on the floor and played with her, her brother, and her sister.

The holidays, primarily a religious celebration in their household, were a time for baking special foods and enjoying family. And a time for sharing.

One Christmas, Eileen and her older sister received a gift in tandem. It's the beautiful buggy that still graces her

living room. The two girls took turns strolling their dolly on the family farm in summer, and inside the house in winter.

They also shared two little tea sets, which through the years got all mixed together. The setting for their teas? This cute handmade table that Eileen's father made for her one year.

Her grandfather also fashioned this chair for her.

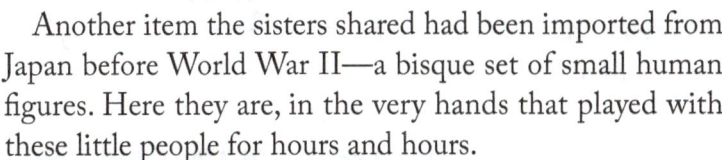

Another item the sisters shared had been imported from Japan before World War II—a bisque set of small human figures. Here they are, in the very hands that played with these little people for hours and hours.

What's left of the fourteen-piece set is shown here, on Eileen's table. And then

there was this woman, whom Eileen recalls being an outsider to the rest of the pretend people as she and her sister made up make-believe scenes.

This doll didn't come with the set, and the girls saw her as an outcast. Interesting, considering her "Oriental" appearance.

Another treasure from those days, this fire engine pull toy came complete with firemen and a bell that no longer rings. But oh, it used to!

Last but not least, this handcrafted dolly crib made by Eileen's father, perhaps for a birthday. Once, it boasted a mattress, pillows, and the works.

Those days are gone, but they hearken back to a time when children gladly shared a gift and took great care of every one they received. Those years when patriotism motivated citizens to tighten their belts give us a glimpse of the strong character built through learning to make do with what one had.

Chapter 8

Celebrating with the Roosevelts

"We may look forward into the future with real, substantial confidence that, however great the cost, 'peace on earth, good will toward men' can be and will be realized and insured."
~President Franklikn D. Roosevelt
Fireside Chat—Christmas Eve, 1943

Christmas at the White House became the bastion of tradition and morale for a nation, an example to citizens of the season's meaning.

The people of the United States, even during the Great Depression, applauded the Roosevelts as they celebrated the season with their children and grandchildren. The president and first lady executed the traditional expressions of Christmas by receiving a tree for the Blue Room, lighting the National Christmas Tree, and ceremoniously blessing the nation.

During the Great Depression, Franklin and Eleanor celebrated with their White House Staff. Their gifts were personal in nature, and memorable. The president's book, *On Our Way*, was autographed and given as a token of appreciation. For several years, pewter pieces such as letter openers, mail organizers, and paperweights were given to the staff. With the arrival of a Scottish terrier, Fala, special

A World War II Holiday Scrapbook

key chains commemorating the dog delighted the workers in the White House.

As president, Franklin always gave a Christmas Eve address, after which he returned to the White House to hear the Washington Choral Society in concert. Then his family joined him in hanging stockings in his bedroom and reading an annotated version of Charles Dickens' iconic novel, *A Christmas Carol.*

On Christmas Day, First Lady Eleanor Roosevelt donated perishable gifts to local charities. Then she visited the underprivileged areas of Washington, DC, sharing gifts, food, and words of encouragement. She ventured to homeless camps in alleys with special presents for these needy souls. One year, she invited Girl Scouts to sing Christmas carols with her at the White House.

Then the attack on Pearl Harbor changed the tenor of the nation. As fear gripped the homeland, the concern for

national defense and public safety became paramount. Traditional events, such as the National Christmas Tree lighting, were challenged as fear of enemy attack lurked on the minds of the military. That year, President Roosevelt and Prime Minister Winston Churchill lit the Christmas tree from the South Portico. The president believed that the message of Christmas would be the country's greatest weapon against our enemies' hatred.

In later war years, the brightly colored bulbs were replaced by ornaments produced by local school children as a wartime conservation measure. A Girl Scout troop gave Eleanor two boxes of ornaments made with peanuts, straws, cotton paper doilies, and red ribbon. Once on the tree, the first lady found the ornaments looked, "very charming and as Christmas-y as anything I have even seen."[1]

Deployment took its toll on the Roosevelt family. All four sons—James, Elliott, Franklin Jr., and John—were recruited into different branches of the Armed Forces. Their daughter, Anna, lived in Seattle Washington and was not able to travel back to the east coast. Now, as empty-nesters without children and grandchildren, the holidays focused on the war effort.

Despite the shortages and rations, Eleanor wanted to give gifts to those she loved. In the third floor solarium, she kept a *Christmas Closet* where she squirreled away presents bought throughout the year in preparation for wrapping in the Yule Tide season. To ensure she bought for everyone, she kept a notebook that listed every year's purchase. A frugal person, she selected tasteful gifts with a budget in mind.

As the war dragged on and resources were scarce, even the White House staff felt the crunch. The gifts under the tree at the White House were unwrapped, because the president wanted to "save paper." In 1942, the employees of the staff received a black leather folder filled with war saving bonds. In 1944, a scroll with FDR's "D-Day Prayer" was given with the signature, "Christmas, 1944—from FDR."

The year 1944 denotes the last Christmas that the nation enjoyed with the Roosevelts. The celebration was low key, but memorable. The National Christmas Tree was "speckled with hundreds of brilliant ornaments contributed by children of Washington." Tinsel for the tree grew thin as tin became difficult to obtain. The US Marine Band played while the people gathered to sing.

True to her nature, First Lady Eleanor visited wounded troops at Walter Reed Hospital, reached out to the poorer neighborhoods, and entered into alleys filled with the homeless. Her cheerful and compassionate spirit brought hope in a dark time in history. Ironically, Eleanor's favorite song was, "Brighten the Corner Where You Are." At Christmas time, she made a special effort to do just that.

The Roosevelts attended a Christmas Service that morning in '44. Eleanor wrote in her "My Day" column: "As I watched some of the boys in uniform, I knew that many of them had come back from far distant places to share this Christmas time with their families…I try to remember always what an old friend of my grandmother's used to say: 'Enjoy every minute you have with those you love, my dear, for no one can take joy that is past away from you. It will be there in your heart to live on when the dark days come.'"[2]

In his study at Hyde Park, FDR gave what would be his final Christmas message to a nation he had led through so many challenges. The armed services overseas listened to his speech over shortwave radio. For over a decade, the nation had hung onto his words of encouragement from his Fireside Chats.

The president stated: "We pray that with victory will come a new day of peace on earth in which all the Nations of the earth will join together for all time. That is the spirit of Christmas, the holy day. May that spirit live and grow throughout the world in all the years to come."[3]

1. "Eleanor Roosevelt's 'My Day': Christmas." by Mary Jo Binker, The Eleanor Roosevelt Project, The White House Historical Association.

2. "My Day," by Eleanor Roosevelt, December 27, 1944.

3. "Christmas with the Roosevelts," by Matthew Costello, Vice President of the Rubenstine Center for White House History, The White House Historical Association.

Chapter 9

Popping Up Some Comfort

Popcorn gained popularity in the times of this nation's duress. During the Great Depression, popcorn satisfied hunger as a cheap snack that the whole family enjoyed. The popcorn industry thrived, moving right into the rations of WWII.

Sugar rations created a shortage of sweet snacks and candy. During the war, Americans consumed three times more popcorn than before the war. When combined with corn syrup or molasses, the sticky treat gave homemakers a healthy food for youngsters to munch. An added source of protein, peanut butter smacked the sweet tooth without forsaking the war effort.

At Christmas time, popcorn and cranberries were threaded onto a string to circle the tree with festive color. As much popcorn probably was eaten as was strung for a garland. But the coziness of a family creating a Christmas decoration together even in a blacked-out living room helped to ease the anxiety of the war. Many Christmas trees boasted colorfully cellophane-wrapped popcorn balls hung as ornaments on sturdy branches.

Popcorn arrived at Christmas in the boxes of goodies that were mailed to the veterans across the ocean. As a packing material that tasted good even after a month of travel, the GIs enjoyed the flavor of a food that signified *home*. Even

Popping Up Some Comfort

stale packing popcorn hugged the young man lying in a foxhole in a foreign country on Christmas Day, testifying to the power of food-memory connection.

During the war, Cracker Jack supplied field and emergency rations for the Allies. In 1943 and 1944, the company received three awards from the Army and Navy, including one for high achievement in the production of materials needed by our armed forces. Soldiers recalled the thrill of getting a box of Cracker Jack in their Trick or Treat bag or stuffed into a Christmas stocking. The drawing of patriotic Sailor Jack and his dog, Bingo, printed on every box, united a lonely military man with his boyhood back in the States. The molasses-flavored, caramel-coated popcorn and peanuts eaten by a lonely GI with gun fire in the distance brought a brief but comforting respite. A K-rations treat was welcomed any day of the year, but maybe more on a nostalgic Christmas Eve.

Popcorn at Christmas time. A garland. A family treat. A GI memory.

RECIPE FOR POPCORN BALLS
By Cathy Korges, Hazen, North Dakota

Ingredients
   7 quarts popped popcorn
   1 cup sugar
   1 cup light corn syrup
   ¼ cup water
   ¼ teaspoon salt
   3 Tablespoons butter
   1 teaspoon vanilla extract

Directions

Place popcorn in a large baking pan; keep warm in a 2oo degree oven.

In a heavy saucepan, combine sugar, corn syrup, water, and salt. Cook over medium heat until a candy thermometer reads 235 degrees (soft-ball stage).

Remove from heat. Add butter, vanilla; still until butter melted. Immediately pour over popcorn and still until evenly coated.

When mixture is cool enough to handle, quickly shape into 3 inch balls, dipping hands in cold water to prevent sticking.

Chapter 10

Deploying Santa and the Reindeer

*"The stockings were hung by the chimney with care,
In hopes that St. Nicholas soon would be there."*
~Clement Clarke Moore
"A Visit from St. Nicholas"

Santa Claus had helped out the nation with the toy issue for decades. Even during the Great Depression, he appeared at churches on Christmas Eve with candy pokes for the children, and nuts and oranges to boot. Now, he and the reindeer were deployed to help with WWII.

The Jolly Old Elf urged Americans to buy war bonds and give them as gifts to friends and family. He demonstrated how to conserve resources. With a finger to his lips, Santa impressed the public on the importance of silence in order to prevent leaks to the enemy.

The importance of Santa to the home front emerged when the War Labor Board ordered on December 4, 1942, that "Bona fide Santa Clauses" were excluded from the wage-freeze order that enveloped most workers. The department-store Santa making $20 a week in 1941 could expect to take home $25 in 1942.

This exemption from the wage freeze "shall not be considered as a precedent, since the role of Santa Claus in a war-torn world is unique." But, to be a "bona fide" Santa, the attire must include "a red robe, white whiskers, and other well-recognized accouterments befitting their station in life."[1]

As women took over formerly male-driven occupations, there still remained one occupation that the public wanted to be filled by a man: department store Santa. The resistance to

Deploying Santa and the Reindeer

women in the position was broken when the public realized that it was a female Santa or no Santa at all.

In 1942, a Chicago department store began using a woman in the role of Santa. The children did not notice any difference.

In the same year, a Woolworth in New Jersey used a Santa who wore a skirt, but kept the white wig and beard. The children told this Santa exactly what to bring to their house on Christmas Eve.

Syndicated columnist Henry McLemore could not get over the feminine Santa, because he didn't think she could carry a heavy sack. Her giggling also caused his ire to rise, but a call for senior citizens of the male gender to fill the gap failed.

By 1943 and 1944, women frequently played Santa, talking with boys and girls who lived in a world of black outs and Black Stars in windows. When 1945 circled around, Santa returned to being a male-dominated job.

Across the ocean, Wiltz, a small town in Luxembourg, was hit hard during the Battle of the Bulge. Houses destroyed, young men conscripted, hope demolished. In 1944, the celebration of St. Nicholas Day drew near.

Harry Stutz and Richard Brookins, corporals in the U.S. Army's 28th Infantry Division, arrived in Wiltz. When they discovered that the parents had no gifts for their children, Stutz and Brookins went into action. Brookins dressed up as St. Nicholas. He recalled: "I didn't know who Saint Nicholas was, so I didn't know what he did, and I didn't want to spoil it for the kids." Donning the local priest's robes, a beard made of rope, a staff and a bishop's miter, he looked the part.

Stutz and Brookins joined with other soldiers in collecting treats from their care packages. On December 5, Brookins was driven by jeep into Wiltz. Two girls dressed as angels flanked him. They visited the town's schools. The children sang and the GIs passed out treats. Brookins learned that "the little ones just ate that up like our kids do with Santa Claus." He was a convincing St. Nicholas.

In 2016, Brookins was presented with the Luxembourg Military Medal, which has also been given to Dwight D. Eisenhower and Winston Churchill. For the people of the devastated town, the Santa-infused American trying to be St. Nicholas made their lives a bit happier in a time of despair.

Saint Nicholas or Santa Claus. Either way, he created a magical moment for children in a time when reality had been harsh. He transformed Christmas into a time to believe.

"But I heard him exclaim, ere he drove out of sight–
'Happy Christmas to all, and to all a good night!'"

---

1. "Here's How Santa Claus Was Rewarded During World War II", By Justin Worland, December 24, 2014, TIME, history/white house.

Chapter 11

Giving from the Heart

"My idea of Christmas, whether old-fashioned or modern, is very simple: loving others."
~Bob Hope

Only the rich had historically given expensive and numerous gifts at Christmas. The vast majority of Americans remembered the leanness of the Great Depression years, and now chaffed under the rationing of materials needed to create toys, clothing or other items worthy of gift giving. In a wartime America, the patriotic duty of each citizen was to contribute to the safety of "our boys."

War bonds headed the list of gift items. An advertisement for war bonds depicted a boy looking excited about getting a bond and contributing to the war effort. Ads even aimed at buying war bonds for soldiers to secure their future when they returned. The push to use bonds as patriotic Christmas gifts proved successful.

In an era when practicality reigned, the gift-giving list between adults reflected a concern for useable presents. Victory Gardens abounded on every bit of soil, so gardening supplies or seeds made a nice package.

Homemade dibbers, those pointed wooden sticks for making holes in the ground, also appealed to the organic side of gift giving. Placed in a clay pot and tied up with useable string, any gardener would be happy to receive such a gift.

Produce from the Victory Gardens was canned using favorite—and sometimes secret—family recipes. Mango-peach salsa, apple chutney, strawberry-rhubarb jam, and Bar B Q sauces sported decorated lids and served as delectable additions to plain and simple foods gleaned on rations. They made for delicious gift trading.

For knitters who could unravel old or outgrown sweaters, the prospect of a set including hat, scarf and gloves brought a smile to a loved one. Quilters gathered scraps of cloth to stitch together comforters for the wintery nights as the country conserved the coal supply. Any efforts to supply added warmth made great Christmas gifts.

One sought-after gift from friends was soap. Yes, soap.

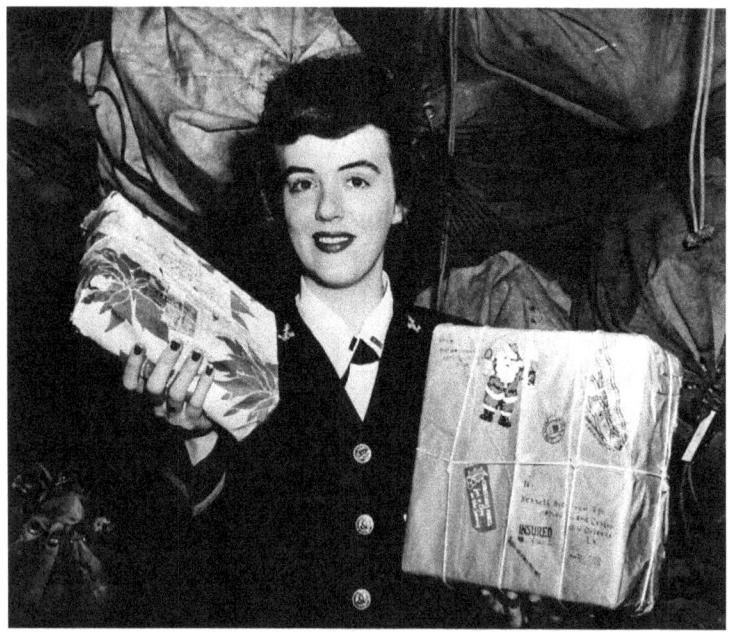

Giving from the Heart

As Clara Milburn wrote in her diary, "never in all my life have I been so short of soap—a nasty feeling." A few bars of homemade soap with specially selected scents or scrubs made a present of ultimate luxury. Most homemakers of the 1940s could whip up a batch of soap in a few hours and infuse it with their own brand of lathering, which made a treat for their friends.

Wrapping paper was an expensive item outside the budget of many. Brown paper or white paper from the grocer or butcher could be decorated with potato prints and used to wrap gifts. The already accepted tradition of wrapping gifts in comics that had dominated the Dust Bowl era was resurrected in WWII. Bits of cloth folded around a small present and tied with a bit of ribbon created the beauty many desired for their Christmas offerings.

Tiny pine cones or bits of pine needles tethered to the gift gave an organic feel to a plain package. When money was short, ingenuity and creativity made a noticeable difference.

Christmas is a time of giving from the heart. An old saying speaks this wisdom. "I learned to give not because I have much, but because I know exactly how it feels to have nothing."

Chapter 12

Innovative Christmas Gifts

"The world has grown weary through the years, but at Christmas, it is young."
~Phillip Brooks

With a war raging, rations squeezing resources, and money tight, it is ironic that the two most sought after children's gifts were developed during World War II.

Even more impressive, these two gifts have remained favorite toys for kids in the succeeding decades. Who would imagine that a rolled-up wire and a slimy lump would satisfy war-weary youngsters?

Christmas holidays seldom dominated the mind of Richard James, a naval engineer. The Navy needed to protect sensitive equipment from the constant motion on ships and boats, so Richard James was diligently working on torsion springs. One fell out of a box. An inquisitive sort, James watched as that spring "walked" across a table.

His mind became intrigued by the possibilities. James spent the next year tinkering with coils. He needed the slinkiest shape, and one fully compressed when relaxed. Finally, he perfected the coil, including the ability of this spring to sort of flow when set in motion.

James and his wife, Betty, borrowed $500 to manufacture the novelty toy. Then James designed a machine to coil 80 feet

Innovative Christmas Gifts

of wire into a two-inch spiral. Betty named the toy "Slinky," and sales were sluggish at first.

Then, Christmas 1945 proved the worth of the Slinky. Gimbels Department Store in Philadelphia allowed Richard James to demonstrate the stair-stepping Slinky. Four hundred Slinkys sold within minutes.

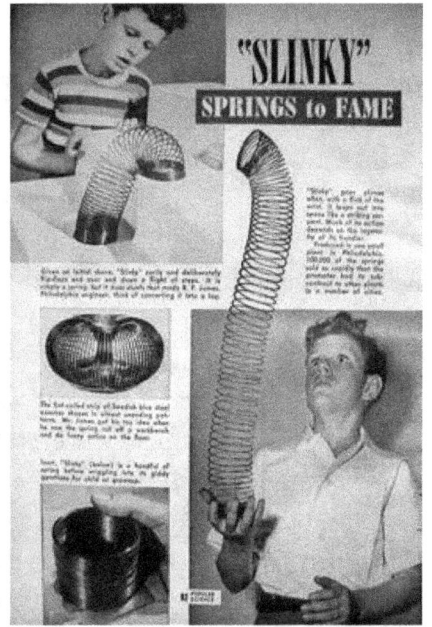

As Betty claimed, "Children love simple things. They're not the only ones." The Slinky headed the wish list of many children who had been "nice" in a year when parents could make only a few Christmas dreams come true.

The Slinky story may remind Christmas shoppers of another account—the tale of Silly Putty. It is told like this.

One of the most important resources needed for WWII was rubber. It was essential for tires, boots, gas masks, life rafts and bombers. The Japanese attacked the rubber-producing countries in Asia, making it hard for America to get this product, so a synthetic needed to be created.

In 1943, James Wright worked in General Electric's laboratory in New Haven, Connecticut. He discovered that, in a test tube, boric acid and silicone oil produced an interesting gob of goo.

Wright conducted tests which showed that this gob could

bounce when dropped, stretch further than rubber, collect no mold and had a high melting temperature. But it could not replicate rubber.

Instead, the "nutty putty" was passed around in parties where neighbors and friends stretched, molded, and dropped the goo to the delight of many. One can assume that it created a hit at several Christmas gatherings of home-front families needing a diversion from the war.

In 1949, Ruth Fallgatter, a toy store owner, put the globs in plastic cases and priced them at two dollars each as "bouncing putty." This toy outsold everything except for a fifty cent Crayola crayon set. The rest of the story is history, especially as Silly Putty served as a stocking stuffer and Secret Santa gift for many youngsters over the years.

Sometimes life has twists and turns in it. From the inventive minds of scientists working to win a war, two favorite children's toys were created.

Now, doesn't that make the holidays bright?

SILLY PUTTY RECIPE

Ingredients
    ½ cup white glue
    ¾ cup water
    1 teaspoon borax

Directions

Dissolve the borax in the water, and then mix it with the glue. Put the resulting polymer in a Ziploc bag and knead it until it forms a nice stretchy mass. Pour the remaining liquid down the drain.

From the Real World Science Curriculum
Rob Walla, STEM Coordinator
at the *National WWII Museum*

Chapter 13

The Fragrance of Yule Tide

"The things you take for granted someone else is praying for."

~Anonymous

The spicy aroma of gingerbread fresh from the oven. The scent of chestnuts roasting on an open fire. The sweet smell of sugar cookies cooling on a rack ready to be frosted. The mouth-watering whiff of turkey being basted. The

The Fragrance of Yule Tide

breath-deepening bouquet from clove studded oranges. These scents all contribute to olfactory overload at Christmas.

Special efforts afforded the troops on military bases and on the front lines a traditional Christmas dinner with all the fixings. The cooks prepared turkey, cranberries, potato salad, hot soup with giblets and rice, steamed pudding with hard sauce, fruit cake, and Danish pastry. Candied carrots or yams, nuts, and olives appeared on some military menus. Bringing that home-cooked flavor to homesick men boosted morale in a war that dragged through five holiday seasons.

In 1942, the troops in Guadalcanal enjoyed an orange and a warm beer. Those serving in combat zones made do with their K-rations.

Some sailors joined the Red Cross to hold Christmas parties. In Europe, 200 Italian orphans were entertained with food and a decorated mop by the ship's crew. Kimberly Guise, assistant director of the National WWII Museum noted: "It was sort of mutually beneficial. They got to provide this normal experience for the young population who had been suffering under wartime conditions and occupation. And they got to celebrate and see young kids."

Preparing for Christmas Dinner on the home front demanded ingenuity. All the ingredients that created the icon foods of the season headed the rationed list, so homemakers saved their sugar and butter coupons. They hoarded tea and coffee. The women used altered recipes for favorite desserts. Dried fruit was hard to get, so bread crumbs and grated carrots bulked out cakes.

Turkeys were sent to the boys on the front, but rabbit, chicken, goose, and lamb remained available at home. As the war progressed, food became "mock." For example, a goose-shaped potato casserole might serve as the main dish.

Because the Victory Gardens produced so abundantly, canned vegetables abounded on the table. Chutneys accompanied the meal, and jams sweetened hot rolls. Pickles and salsas added zip for the taste buds. Root vegetables like carrots and turnips baked up into delicious side dishes. As

Freedom from Want

The Fragrance of Yule Tide

always, an empty chair awaited someone who was missing from the table.

For many, a whiff of pumpkin pies sets off a host of memories. Times of emergency intensify the appreciation for the tastes and aromas of favorite foods. Less is required to satisfy that feeling of family and home—just the scent of Christmas dinner will do.

"The smells of Christmas are the smells of childhood"
                                    -Richard Paul Evans

APPLE PAN DOWDY
Modified from The Victory Cook Book, 1942
Published by The Household Science Institute, Chicago

Apple Filling
   5 apples
   Pinch of salt
   2/3 cup molasses
   1/3 tsp. apple cider vinegar
   1/2 teaspoon cinnamon

Directions

Preheat oven to 450 degrees. Peel, core and quarter apples. Mix with other filling ingredients. Pour apple mixture into an 8 inch cast iron pan. Place in oven for 15 minutes

Biscuit Topping
   1 and 1/2 cups flour
   1/4 teaspoon salt
   3 and 1/2 teaspoon baking powder
   4 Tablespoons of cold shortening
   2/3 cup milk
   1 Tablespoon honey

Directions

Mix together dry ingredients. Cut in shortening until it is in pea-sized chunks. Slowly add milk to make a wet dough. Mix until just combined. Place mixture on top of the apple-molasses and return to oven for 20 minutes or until biscuit dough is golden brown on top. Serve warm with heavy cream, if available. Makes a delicious left over.

The Fragrance of Yule Tide

WACs and the Holidays

Cpl. Natalie D. Sceets was born in Wauwatosa, Wisconsin in 1920 and lived there until she joined the WACs. After training in Des Moines Iowa, she was stationed at Avon Park Air Base in Florida in the Corporal Squadron W 325th Army Air Forces Base Unit.

In her original enlistment paperwork, she requested to be a Link Simulator, but served as an Air Operations Specialist. Possibly Avon Park had no slot for a Link Simulator at the time.

In her Specialist role, she assisted in the administration of an air forces operations office. This included keeping records of flying time, assigned aircraft, and the condition of aircraft. She was responsible for initiating maintenance work on planes and directed students as to when to land or take off from the airport.

Natalie and her comrades had fun, too. They kept the spirit of Christmas, as this invitation evidences.

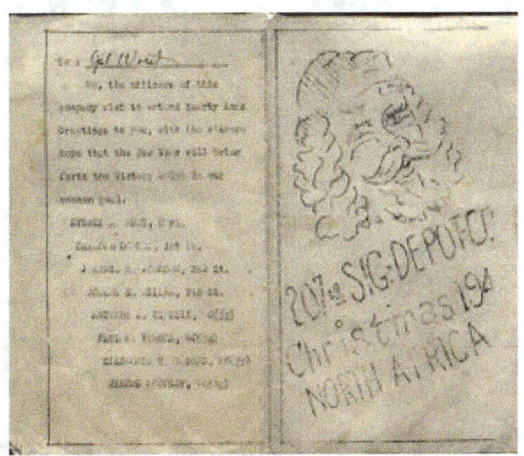

Chapter 14

The Red Cross Christmas Parcels

"She had discovered within herself the unlikely gift for functioning with equilibrium and efficiency inside a full-blown, unending nightmare."
~A Red Cross worker during WWII in Italy

The Red Cross went into action even before the United States entered the conflict in WWII. In 1939, the Red Cross became the chief provider of relief supplies for civilian victims in Europe. In February 1941, the Red Cross began a Blood Donor Service for plasma for the armed forces. After the

The Red Cross Christmas Parcels

attack on Pearl Harbor on December 7, 1941, the organization mobilized "as a medium between the people of the United States of America and their Army and Navy."

By 1945, 7.5 million Red Cross volunteers worked along with 39,000 staff to serve 16 million military personnel, including one million combat casualties. Nearly every family in America contained a member who had either served as a Red Cross volunteer, made contributions of money or blood, or was a recipient of Red Cross services.

One notable group of Red Cross volunteers were the Donut Dollies who traveled with American soldiers. These energetic college grads fried donuts and dodged bombs as

they served the troops from Clubmobiles. Their Red Cross trucks followed the troops across France and Belgium, helping the soldiers through the holidays with a connection to home and patriotism.

The Red Cross's work was never as important as at Christmas. In 1944, with troops about to enter into the Battle of the Bulge, other American soldiers who had been captured by the Germans languished in POW camps across Europe. These prisoners faced a lonely Christmas.

At the well-established camps, prisoners of war were allowed to receive Christmas parcels. The American Red Cross packed and shipped 75,000 Christmas packages in the summer of 1944, hoping for a timely arrival. These treasured packages contained tobacco, games, some seasonal decorations, and a mixture of canned food including canned turkey, jam, Vienna sausage, and fruit cake.

Stalag Luft III allowed the POWs to roam the grounds on Christmas Eve and Christmas day. Concerts and services filled the time, and the auditorium which held 700 men. Not all the 11,000 prisoners could see the Christmas pageant, even with multiple performances.

In Stalag VIIA, the guards brought small pine trees. The men decorated them with snowflakes cut from tin cans, food labels and nails. They savored food from their shared Red Cross packages.

Second Lieutenant Julian J. Gates enlisted in the Army Air Corps and was captured on April 9, 1942, one of the men on Bataan Death March. As the war dragged on, Gates kept a diary. He speaks of receiving two Red Cross parcels for three men to share. The hungry GIs appreciated the food in those packages.

The Red Cross Christmas Parcels

They cut newspapers into strips for a chain to hang around their room. Then they cut tin cans into narrow strips to hang as tinsel from the ceiling. Wreaths were made with pine needles collected from the camp. The men sang carols and enjoyed the hope of the Christmas message.

On Christmas Day, 1943, Gates reflected on his third Christmas far away from home. "I can certainly say that this has been my grandest Xmas since a prisoner because any one of the 768 POWs could have and did get full of food. Also, because to a man we know next Xmas will find us at home." The camp was freed on September 2, 1945.[1]

On Christmas Eve, 1944, the Red Cross teamed up with Fifth Army Montecatini, Italy to hold a Christmas Party for about 200 Italian orphans. Both soldiers and children entered into the joy of the season, when "peace on earth" seemed a possibility. Any break in the war helped the men and children to survive.

A World War II Holiday Scrapbook

During the holiday time in 1943, American soldiers endured cold, muddy conditions in Italy. Noted war correspondent Ernie Pyle wrote that "our troops were living in almost inconceivable misery… Thousands of men had not been dry in weeks."

In such circumstances, a Red Cross package would make the day a bit more manageable.

During Christmas 1944, Allied troops fought the Battle of the Bulge in one of the worst winters in decades. James Lambeth, 37th Amphibious Combat Engineer remembers. "It was the middle of winter, with freezing temperatures and snow on the ground. We sat in foxholes for most of the time, shivering and shaking. One of my buddies and I got in one foxhole and put our backs together, to keep from freezing."[2]

The 1944 Christmas ad for the Red Cross reads: "Your Red Cross will be at his side this Christmas. Remember the dollars you gave to the Red Cross last March? Now they're saying 'Merry Christmas' to American boys all over the world. At old-fashioned Christmas parties in Red Cross clubs and in hospital wards. At prison camps, where the men get special Red Cross gift packages. And at front lines, where the Red Cross goes through fire to deliver Christmas boxes to men in foxholes and at isolated gun posts. Wherever your boy is, you are with him…through your Red Cross."

The Red Cross Christmas Parcels

"The greatest heroes of the Normandy battlefield were the unarmed medics, whom snipers often shot at despite their Red Cross armbands."

~Antony Beevor
English military historian and author

1. "Christmas in a World War II POW Camp," by Morgan Byrn, Tennessee State Museum Quarterly Newsletter.
2. "WWII troops spent Christmas in the field." By Tom Emery for Daily News, December 24, 2019.

Chapter 15

When War Changes the Pulpit

"Surrounded by hundreds of his equally doomed shipmates, the red blinking lights of their life preservers reminded him of Christmas lights."
~First Sergeant Michael Warish
survivor of USAT Dorchester, February 3, 1943

In his article, "'I had all that I needed': Christmas 1944,'" John Wukovits documents the accounts of the graduates from Notre Dame University as they ministered to American troops in conflict zones. Wukovits writes extensively about these priests in his book, *Soldiers of a Different Cloth*.

The chaplains from Notre Dame University served with courage and distinction during WWII. Father Thomas A. Steiner headed 35 priests and missionaries as they deployed overseas. He wrote: "Our chaplains are pretty well scattered over the face of the earth. They are on all fronts except the Russian front. When they all get back there will be no country and no island that some one of them have not been on, or at least, have had a close look at."[1]

For the chaplains serving in Europe and the Pacific, Steiner advised. "Keep up your courage, and frequently renew your confidence in Divine Providence. You are doing God's work." He did not know how much his priests needed those words as they faced a war that would make them question their faith.

When War Changes the Pulpit

The Christmas of 1944 brought familiar yearnings for home and tradition. But the celebration of the birth of the Prince of Peace in the midst of the evil that the troops encountered daily chipped at the priests' resolve. They wanted to deepen the Christmas message to the GIs who faced death and give them courage.

Father Joseph Barry spent several years with the 157th Regiment of the 45th Infantry Division in the Vosges Mountains of France. Christmas would be celebrated in snow-covered foxholes. To these tired and weary men, Barry spoke about leaning on their faith to get through adversity. Even to him, the words seemed empty. He prayed that the men around him would hang onto their belief.

Barry could always be found at the front, dodging bullets and shells as he comforted terrified young men. With the holidays approaching, he begged his friends back home in his letters: "Do say an earnest prayer for the boys fighting along this western front. The boys have a word for it—'plenty rough.'"[2] Celebrating Christmas in a place of physical danger brought new meaning to the holiday for Father Barry.

Four hundred Americans were captured during the early days of the Battle of the Bulge. Father Francis Sampson from Des Moines, Iowa, trekked out of Belgium to a German prison camp in that group. The prisoners marched on Christmas Eve until dark with no food, hoping to stay alive. The Germans had a Christmas feast of half a boiled turnip, half a slice of bread and a cup of warm water waiting for each of them. Grumbling moved through the ranks.

To quell the anger of the detainees, Sampson and the American colonel in charge conducted a Christmas service. The men sang "Silent Night." After a prayer and short sermon,

Sampson reminded the hushed captives that even in a prison camp, Christ was with them. The men settled down, but Sampson knew his work had just begun.

In the Pacific Ocean, Father Henry Heintskill ministered to the men on the escort carrier USS Tulagi. On Christmas Eve, he heard two sailors hum "Silent Night" in off-key vigor. He wrote: "You somehow feel that tonight our lookouts are not the best in the world. Somehow you feel that even though they're looking up toward the sky their eyes are staring off into the blackness back toward their homes."[3]

Homesickness at Christmas overtook the rank and file. Far from family and traditions, the GIs learned a foundational truth. In the words of Freya Stark, *"Christmas is a piece of home that one carries in one's heart."* Father Heintskill saw that truth in the eyes of the sailors aboard the USS Tulagi.

Father John Dupuis, who accompanied the 4th Marine Division, brushed the grime from the front lines off his fatigues. Then he preached to 1,500 Marines at Midnight Mass on a back base in the Pacific theatre. The truth of the gospel gave him the strength he needed to minister to these troops.

For three years, Brother Rex Hennel, two priests, two brothers and two nuns had been confined to a Philippine prison camp. In 1944, they decided to lift spirits with a Midnight Mass in the barracks chapel, and singing Christmas carols and hymns in a multi-faith service.

These people of the cloth considered this the happiest of Christmases. Father Hennel spoke for all of them. "Sitting quietly before the Blessed Sacrament with the whole of my possessions on me—a pair of shorts and a pair of sandals—I fully realized I had all I needed." A deep lesson for a chaplain to carry through life.

Perhaps the experience of Private John Hogan expresses what many GIs felt as they worshipped with their chaplains in foreign countries. Hogan spent Christmas in Hawaii after fighting in the Aleutian Islands.

"You can picture ten or fifteen of us 'rugged' soldiers gathered around in our tent singing 'Away in a Manger'. As we sang, my eye traveled around the tent walls where our rifles hung in readiness as grim reminders of the world as it is. And I thought of how completely and infinitely greater is the power of Christ than the power of the world, and of the symbol of the manger that will endure in time long after war and destruction and material things have passed away. I know that the Cradle will outlast the cannon."[4]

The priests from Notre Dame survived the war with distinction and service to mankind. They demonstrated the compassion and endurance of all chaplains of all denominations who lived with the military in the roughest and most dangerous of conditions. These men and women of faith demonstrate the best that our nation has to offer, and they bring the message of Christmas to all.

Peace on Earth and Goodwill to Man.

> *"We ought to love when others hate...we can bring faith where doubt threatens; we can awaken hope where despair exists; we can light up a light where darkness reigns; we can bring joy where sorrow dominates."*

Those words, as well as any, represent the lessons of The Four Chaplains: a Catholic, a Jew and two Protestants who

put others before self as the Dorchester sank in the freezing waters of the North Atlantic.
~U-233 first officer, Gerhard Buske.

"I had all that I needed," Christmas 1944, by John Wukovits, December 18, 2017, *Notre Dame Magazine*, University of Notre Dame.
Page 1

Page 3

Page 4

"Beyond the Battle: Religion and American Troops in World War II," by Kevin L. Walters, University of Kentucky, Theses and Dissertations- History, 2013, page177.

Chapter 16

That Homesick Feeling

Home for the holidays, *for snow and mistletoe,* as Bing Crosby crooned in the hit Christmas song, "I'll be Home for Christmas." Instilled in each person are the customs of their family, community, and religion. The familiarity of performing the same ceremonies each year brings security. The lighting of the Christmas tree, ice skating at the pond on Christmas Day, exchanging gifts, baking special cookies, candlelight, or bringing in pine laden branches to decorate.

A World War II Holiday Scrapbook

As the soldiers lay on their cots or kept their heads down in a foxhole, these traditions waved through them with eye watering memories.

Home for the sounds of Christmas. Fortunately, the Armed Forces Radio Services with Bing Crosby produced programs and music for the troops. Songs like *White Christmas, Chestnuts Roasting on an Open Fire, Have Yourself a Merry Little Christmas*, and *Happy Holidays* brought the nostalgia of home to the front, producing a melancholy sing-along for many.

The music of the season also varied with the home town of the military personnel. Those from big cities missed hearing

the orchestras play Handel's *Messiah*. Small town soldiers longed for the school pageant with young siblings dressed in bathrobes singing *Away in a Manger*. From the Appalachian Mountains, the strum of a dulcimer bringing *I Wonder as I Wander* to life would have brought peace to a sailor. Many missed carolers in the streets, singing hymns from door to door.

Home for the church services and family. Christmas Eve and Christmas morning were times when the family dressed up and attended church together to ponder the meaning of the season.

For those entrenched overseas in the war, there would be no Christmas truce like there had been during the First World War. Especially in 1944, American soldiers hunkered in and celebrated the best they could during the Battle of the Bulge and the Siege of Bastogne.

For American soldiers within Bastogne, Christmas services were held by the Army Chaplain. For the soldiers on the battlefield outside the city limits, their hearts became the sanctuary for worship and remembrance of the birth of the Prince of Peace. Even in the midst of shelling, they took time for personal reflection on the meaning of the day.

Belgian families took in some troops. "We were out in the outskirts of Bastogne, we found this farmhouse…Inside was a man and woman, and a little boy and a little girl…the wife, she gave us some soup and black bread. We stayed there all night in this farmhouse. The war was going on fiercely outside, (but) the farmhouse never got hit. We were there Christmas Eve. We sang Christmas songs with this Belgian family: *Jingle Bells* and *Silent Night*. The words were different, but the music was the same."[1]

In the simplicity of sharing, the true spirit of Christmas filled these soldiers with comfort and hope.

On December 24, 1942, Rev. Fred Gehring, a Catholic priest from Brooklyn, New York joined Barney Ross, a Jewish boxer from Chicago to bring hope and build morale. Amid the foxholes of Guadalcanal, Gehring and Ross held a midnight Mass service for their fellow soldiers in B Company, 1st Battalion, 8th Marine Regiment. Ross learned to play Christmas carols on a violin, and Gehring tickled the ivory on an organ. Men from so many different stations and backgrounds sang in unison, making this a Christmas Eve to

That Homesick Feeling

remember because the birth of Jesus brings the promise of an eternal home after this earthly home has ended.[2]

Meanwhile, the most frequently sung tune during the war only intensified the lonely, empty feeling of being separated from all that had been familiar. As Bing Cosby crooned about being home for Christmas in his dreams, tears fell on the home front as well as overseas.

1. "Christmas in Wartime: Battle of the Bulge," by Kaitlyn Crain Enriquez, December 19, 2016, National Archives, The Unwritten Record.
2. "Looking for a Christmas lesson in tolerance? Here's on from the foxholes of WWII in 1942," By Ron Grossman, Chicago Tribune, December 24, 2019.

Photos from National Archives and Records Administration

Special Thanks

The authors would like to extend special thanks to the family of WWII veteran Cpl Natalie D. Sceets and to Eileen Kittleson for their stories and personal photos.

About the Author

Words have always been comfort food for Gail Kittleson. After instructing expository writing and English as a Second Language, she began writing seriously. Intrigued by the World War II era, Gail creates women's historical fiction from her northern Iowa home and also facilitates writing workshops/retreats.

She and her husband, a retired Army chaplain, enjoy their grandchildren and in winter, Arizona's Mogollon Rim Country. You can count on Gail's heroines to ask honest questions, act with integrity, grow in faith, and face hardships with spunk.

Visit Gail online at: GailKittleson.com

About the Author

For 26 years, Cleo Lampos used storytelling, biography and history to reach her classrooms of students in the public schools. Currently, she employs the same techniques to mesmerize senior citizens in community college extension classes.

With a Bachelor's Degree in Education from University of Wisconsin-Whitewater and Master's Degree in Special Education from St. Xavier University-Chicago, Lampos has written seven books and numerous magazine articles. She lives in the Chicago, Illinois area where she quilts, joins her husband in urban gardening, and enjoys her eleven grandchildren.

Visit Cleo online at: CleoLampos.com

Also Available From

WordCrafts Press

All My Goodbyes
  by Jan Cline

Before History Dies
  by Jacob Carter

Saturday & the Witch Woman
  by Dr. Thomas O. Ott

The Rose and the Whip
  by Jae Hodges

Angela's Treasures
  by Marian Rizzo

www.wordcrafts.net